STUART
Skin
Prep
Bowater-Scott
POND'S
cream
cocoa
butter

Franklin Watts
12a Golden Square
London W1R 4BA

Franklin Watts Australia
14 Mars Road
Lane Cove
N.S.W. 2066

ISBN: 0 86313 821 7

Design: Edward Kinsey
Typesetting: Lineage, Watford
Printed in Italy
by G. Canale & C.S.p.A, Turin

The publishers, author and photographer would like to thank Dr Christine Hoyte and her colleagues for their help in the preparation of this book.

Doctor

Tim Wood
Photographs: Chris Fairclough

Franklin Watts
London · New York · Sydney · Toronto

I am a doctor.

I arrive at the surgery early in the morning.

I check the list to find out who has made an appointment to see me.

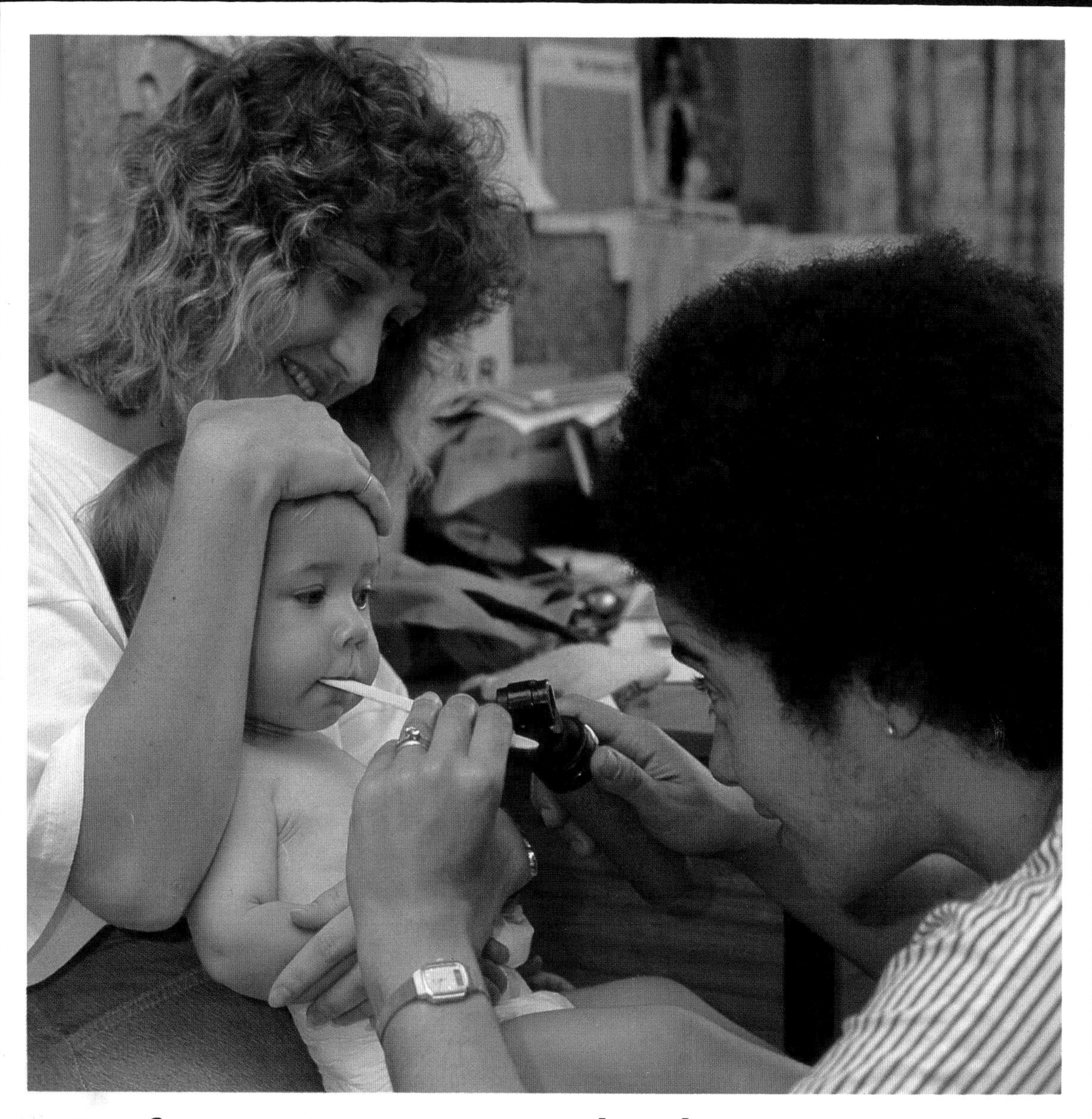

My first patient is a baby.
I examine his throat.

Then I look in his ear.

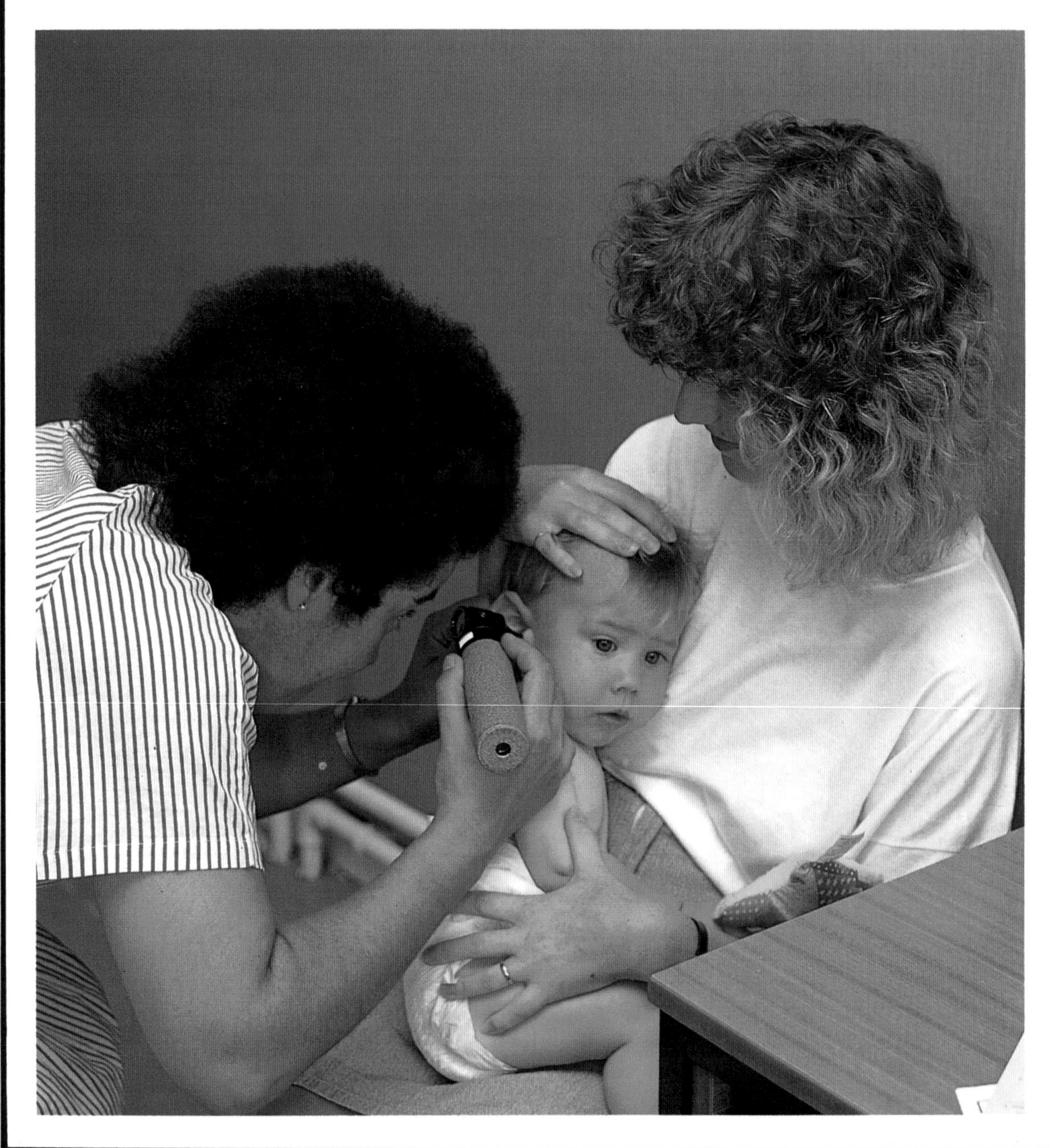

I take
this patient's blood pressure.

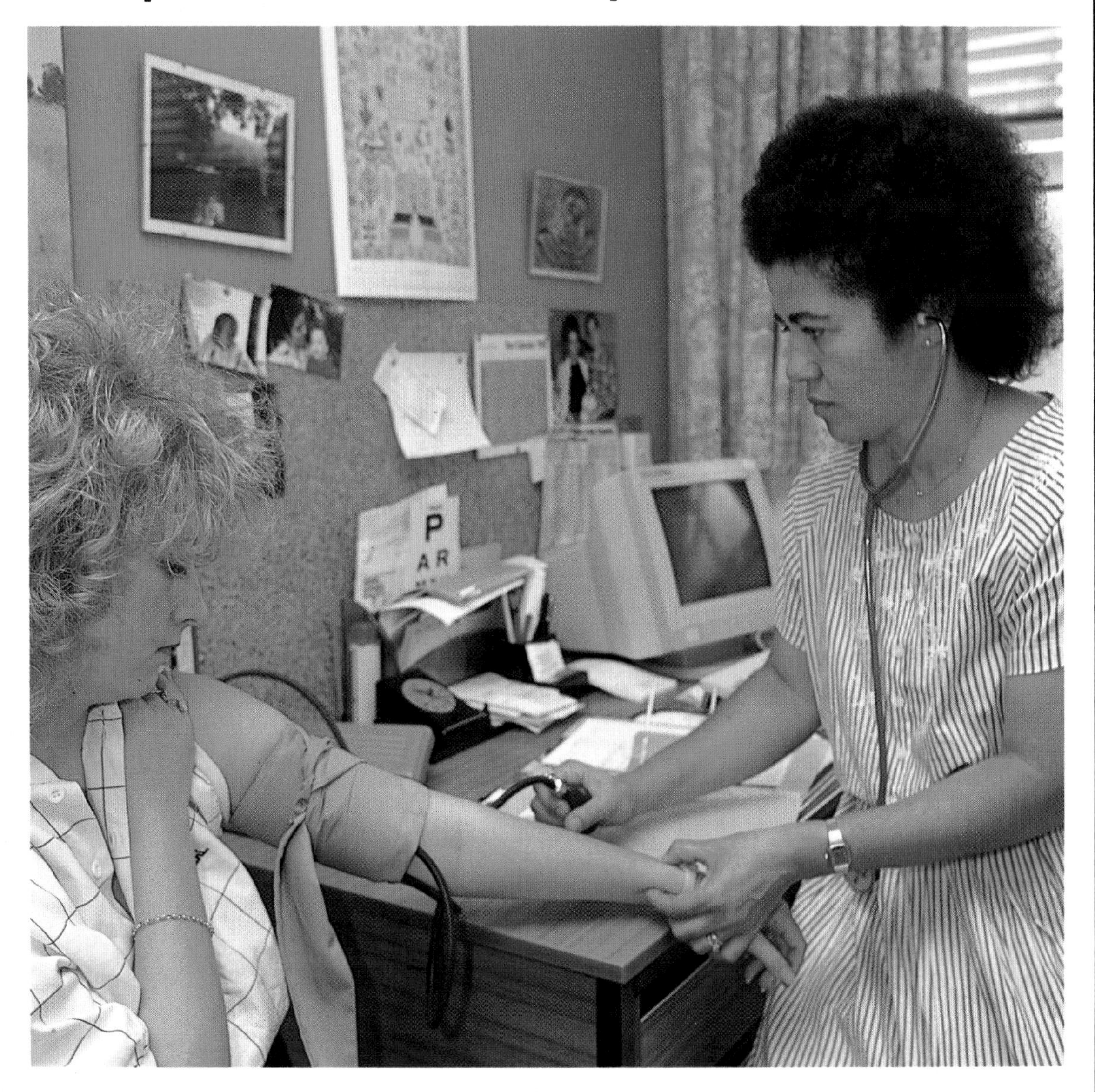

I type a prescription on my computer.

I talk about a patient with the district nurse.

After morning surgery,
I have a coffee break
with the other doctors.

Every patient has a record card.
I have to keep these up to date.

I dictate a letter about a patient into my recording machine.

Sometimes patients ring the surgery asking for advice.

At the end of the morning, I pack my instruments into my bag and go home for lunch.

The surgery rings me at home to tell me about a patient who is ill.

I drive to the patient's house.
Her sister tells me what is wrong.

I make sure that the patient has the right medicine.

I visit another patient.
I test his reflexes.

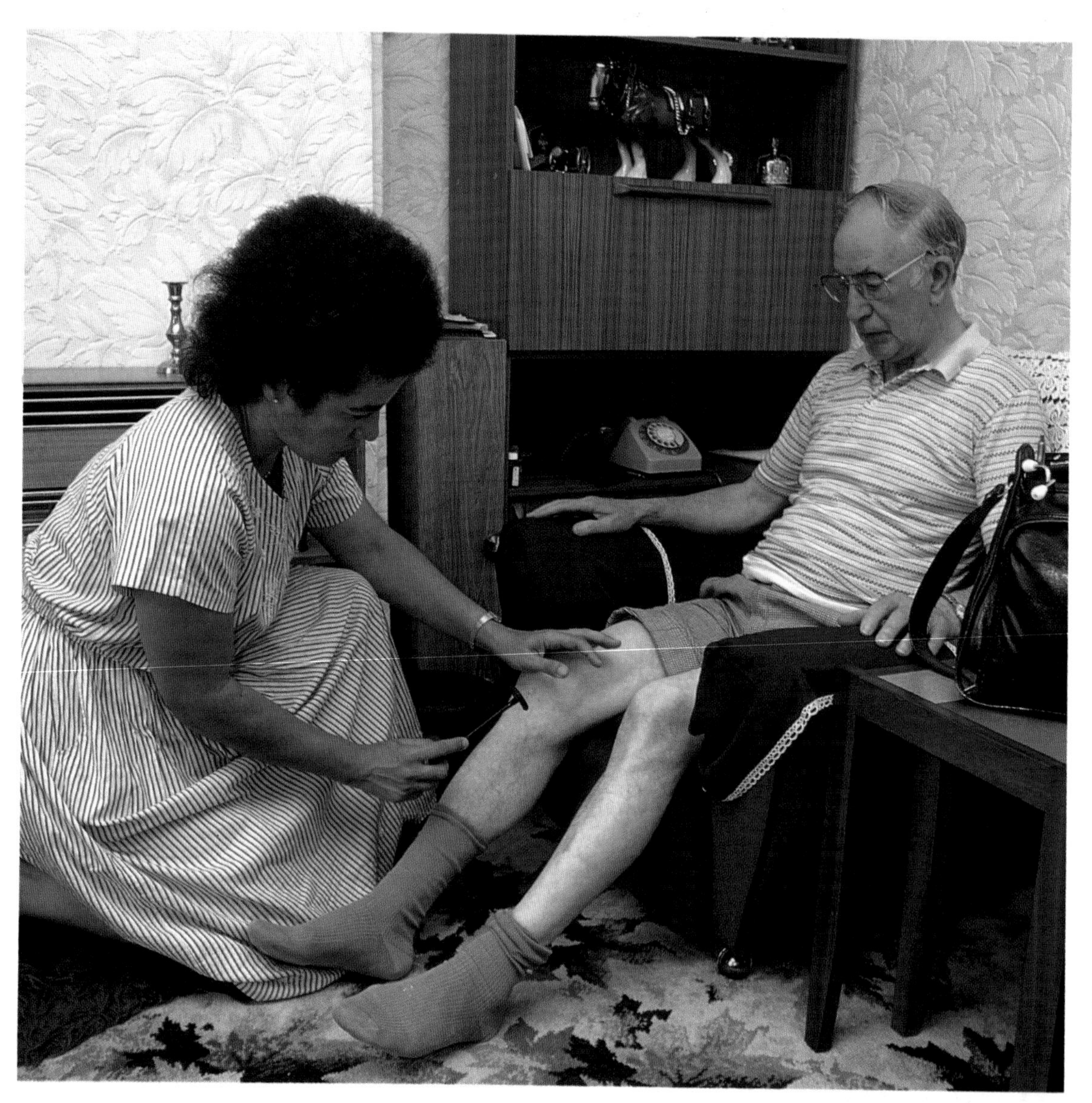

I telephone the surgery
to find out if anyone else
has asked me to visit them.

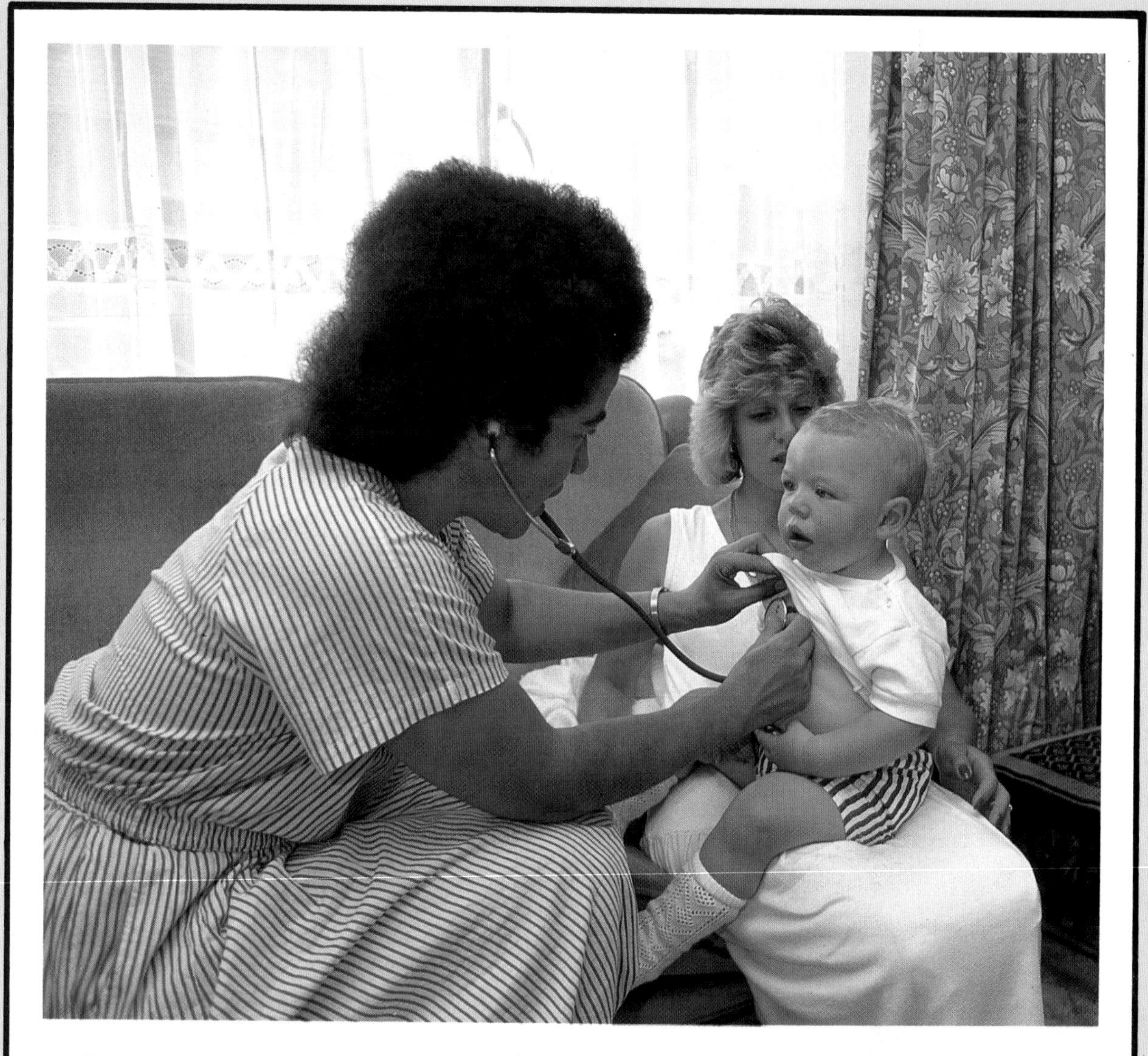

This baby has been coughing.
I listen to his chest
with my stethoscope.

When I have finished my visits,
I go back for evening surgery.

FACTS ABOUT DOCTORS

It takes six years of training to become a doctor. Student doctors study for five years at a medical school or teaching hospital. They then work full-time in a hospital for a year. After that, they can choose to specialise either in hospital or in General Practice (being a family doctor).

There are three full-time doctors and one trainee doctor at the surgery shown in this book. The doctors take it in turns to be "on call" (on duty and ready to visit patients at home).

The three doctors have nearly 6,200 patients to look after in their area.

There are ten other part-time staff at this surgery. These include secretaries, who keep the record cards in order and arrange appointments, and two nurses, who give treatment, make tests and dress wounds.

The National Health Service, run by the government, provides most of the money needed to pay all the staff.

GLOSSARY

Appointment
An arrangement made by a patient to see the doctor at the surgery.

Blood pressure
The force with which blood is pumped around the body by the heart. Measuring blood pressure tells the doctor how well a patient's heart is working.

District nurse
A nurse who visits patients in their own homes.

Prescription
An official note to a chemist which must be presented by a patient when buying certain medicines.

Record card
A list of past illnesses and treatments received by a patient.

Reflexes
Muscle actions. Testing a patient's reflexes is a way for the doctor to check that the muscles and the nerves are working properly.

Stethoscope
An instrument for listening to the heart and lungs.

Surgery
A building where patients come to visit the doctor.

INDEX

Nebuhaler
T0077014
ANAPHYLAXIS
Washing
Liquid